The Appointed Times, the Messiah and the Hebrew Calendar

A Companion Guide to What's Up with the New Moon?

מועד

Rosh Chodesh
Head of the Month

Moedim
Appointed Times

Shabbath Shabbaton

Passover Feast of Unleavened Bread
Wave-sheaf   Feast of Weeks
Day of Trumpets Day of Atonement Feast of Tabernacles

Tracy Huey

Published by Faith That Is His (FTIH)
FaithThatIsHis.com

ISBN 978-1-7337191-5-5

Printed in the United States of America - Updated Edition

Scripture is taken from and based on the King James Version of the Bible. (KJV)

To match the original text more closely, the author uses Yahweh and YHWH instead of the LORD. Elohim instead of God. Yeshua instead of Jesus. Messiah instead of Christ.

Note: This book is nonfiction and contains the views and opinions of the author. This book is intended to provide helpful and informative material on the subject matter covered. The publisher and the author assume no responsibility for any inaccuracies, omissions, errors, or inconsistencies. This book was produced with the full recognition and understanding that the publisher and the author are not liable for the misuse or misconception of the information provided.

Contents

There are several different calendars among those that celebrate the biblical feasts. The enemy will be up to his typical schemes of using our differences to try and divide us. But let us focus on what we have in common. We are celebrating the biblical feasts.

Please No Wolves.

If there ever is anything that takes your eyes off of Yeshua, please look the other way.

How to read the calendars.

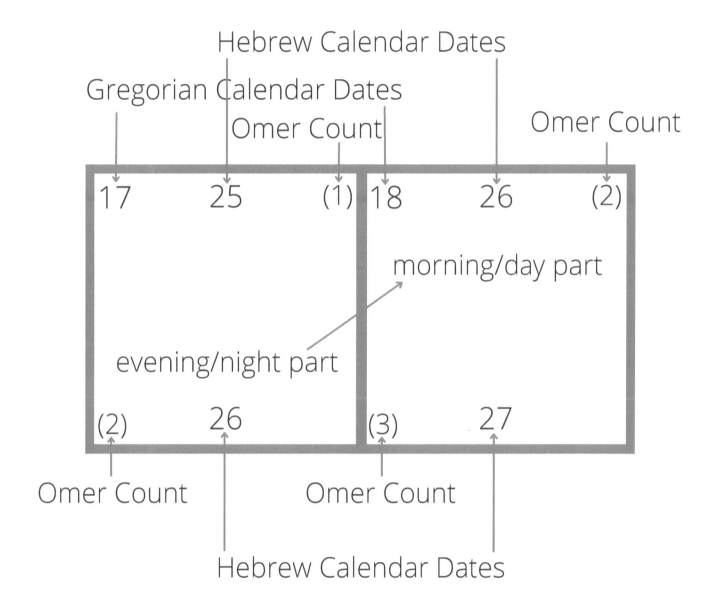

Always looking unto Yeshua.

Leviticus 23:4

These are the feasts (moed) of Yahweh, even holy convocations, which ye shall proclaim in their seasons (moed).

#4150 Moed(im): appointed time, place, or meeting (season)
#6944 Qodesh: apartness, sacredness #4744 Miqra: convocation, convoking, reading (also a rehearsal)
#2282 Chag: a festival gathering, feast, pilgrim feast

The Sabbath is a Moed and a Qodesh Miqra.
The Sabbath is **not** a Chag.

The Passover is a Moed.
The Passover is **not** specified as a Qodesh Miqra, and it is **not** a Chag.

The Feast of Unleavened Bread is a Moed and the 1st and 7th days are Qodesh Miqra.
The Feast of Unleavened Bread is a Chag.

The Wave-sheaf is a Moed.
The Wave-sheaf is **not** specified as a Qodesh Miqra, and it is **not** a Chag.

The Feast of Weeks is a Moed and a Qodesh Miqra.
The Feast of Weeks is a Chag.

The Day of Trumpets is a Moed and a Qodesh Miqra.
The Day of Trumpets is **not** a Chag.

The Day of Atonement is a Moed and a Qodesh Miqra.
The Day of Atonement is **not** a Chag.

The Feast of Tabernacles is a Moed and the 1st and 8th days are Qodesh Miqra.
The Feast of Tabernacles is a Chag.

Always looking unto Yeshua.

1st Day Sunday	2nd Day Monday	3rd Day Tuesday	4th Day Wednesday	5th Day Thursday	6th Day Friday	Shabbat Saturday
17 March **A day begins and ends @ sunset.**	18	19 Spring 19th/20th (see pg. 4) (Latter Rains) Joel 2:23, Jer 5:24 & Dt 11:14	20 **Abib** Year begins @ sunset 1st chodesh / month **1**	21 **1** **2**	22 Shabbat begins @ sunset **3**	23 **3** Shabbath Shabbath Shabbat ends @ sunset **4**
24 **5**	25 **6**	26 **7**	27 **8**	28 **9**	29 **10**	30 **10** Shabbath Shabbathon **11**
31 **12**	1 April **13**	2 Passover begins @ sunset ends @ sunset **14th**	3 **14th** Yeshua crucified Yeshua laid in the tomb **1st Day of the Feast of Unleavened Bread** begins @ sunset **15th**	4 **15th** a night to be much observed Ex 12:42 ends @ sunset **16** no servile work	5 **17**	6 **17th** Yeshua rose from the grave on the Sabbath day Shabbath Shabbathon **18**
7 **18th** Yeshua appeared to Mary and the disciples **19**	8 **20**	9 7th Day of the Feast of Unleavened Bread begins @ sunset **21st**	10 **21st** ends @ sunset **22** no servile work	11 **23**	12 **24**	13 **24** Shabbath Shabbathon (1) **25th**
14 **25th** (1) wave-sheaf 8 days later, Yeshua again appeared to the disciples (2) **26**	15 count (2) until sunset (3) **27**	16 count (3) until sunset (4) **28**	17 count (4) until sunset (5) **29**	18 count (5) until sunset (6) **30**	19 30 count (6) until sunset 2nd chodesh / month begins @ sunset **1**	20 **1** Morrow after the Sabbath - Begin count @ sunset

count (2) begins @ sunset
count (1) until sunset

*Exodus 12:42 It is a **night** to be much observed unto YHWH...* observed #8107 shimmur: a watching, vigil

The 1st Day of the Feast of Unleavened Bread (a high holy day) is also **a night to be much observed** and calls for one to be awake.

NOTE: The Passover (lamb or goat) was slaughtered on the 14th of Abib (Wednesday) prior to sunset. The Passover meal was then prepared and eaten in haste after sunset on the 15th of Abib, the first day of the Feast of Unleavened Bread and a night to be much observed.

Spring

March 19, 2024 10:06pm CDT / March 20, 2024 5:06am IST (Israel Standard Time)

Deuteronomy 11:14 That I will give *you* the rain of your land in his due season, **the first rain (#3138)** and **the latter rain (#4456)**, that thou mayest gather in thy corn, and thy wine, and thine oil. KJV

Jeremiah 5:24 Neither say they in their heart, Let us now fear the LORD (YHWH) our God (Elohim), that given rain, both **the former (#3138)** and **the latter (#4456)**, in his season: he reserveth unto us the appointed weeks of the harvest. KJV

Joel 2:23 Be glad then, ye children of Zion, and rejoice in the LORD (YHWH) your God (Elohim): for he hath given you **the former rain (#4175)** moderately, and he will cause to come down for you the rain, **the former rain (#4175)**, and **the latter rain (#4456)** in the first *month*. KJV

Zechariah 10:1 Ask ye of the LORD (YHWH) rain in the time of **the latter rain (#4456)**; so the LORD (YHWH) shall make bright clouds, and give them showers of rain, to every one grass in the field. KJV

#3138 yowreh: first rain, (former) rain / the early rain (autumn)

#4175 mowreh: (early) rain (mowreh is also used for teacher)

#4456 malqowsh: latter rain (spring rain)

Exodus 12:42 It *is* a night to be much observed unto the LORD (YHWH) for bringing them out from the land of Egypt: this *is* that night of the LORD to be observed of all the children of Israel in their generations. KJV

April / May ו 2nd month 2024

1st Day Sunday	2nd Day Monday	3rd Day Tuesday	4th Day Wednesday	5th Day Thursday	6th Day Friday	Shabbat Saturday
			18	19 April	19 30	20 1 count (7) until sunset
			Begin counting the Sabbaths ———		2nd chodesh / month begins @ sunset	1st Sabbath Shabbath Shabbathon
				30	(7) 1	(8) 2
21 (8)	22 (9)	23 (10)	24 (11)	25 (12)	26 (13)	27 8 (14)
						2nd Sabbath Shabbath Shabbathon
(9) 3	(10) 4	(11) 5	(12) 6	(13) 7	(14) 8	(15) 9
28 (15)	29 (16)	30 (17)	1 (18) May	2 (19)	3 (20)	4 15 (21)
						3rd Sabbath Shabbath Shabbathon
(16) 10	(17) 11	(18) 12	(19) 13	(20) 14	(21) 15	(22) 16
5 (22)	6 (23)	7 (24)	8 (25)	9 (26)	10 (27)	11 22 (28)
						4th Sabbath Shabbath Shabbathon
(23) 17	(24) 18	(25) 19	(26) 20	(27) 21	(28) 22	(29) 23
12 (29)	13 (30)	14 (31)	15 (32)	16 (33)	17 (34)	18 29 (35)
						5th Sabbath Shabbath Shabbathon
(30) 24	(31) 25	(32) 26	(33) 27	(34) 28	(35) 29	(36) 30

_____

_____

_____

_____

1st Day Sunday	2nd Day Monday	3rd Day Tuesday	4th Day Wednesday	5th Day Thursday	6th Day Friday	Shabbat Saturday
19 30 (36) May 3rd chodesh / month begins @ sunset (37) 1	20 1 (37) (38) 2	21 (38) (39) 3	22 (39) (40) 4	23 (40) (41) 5	24 (41) (42) 6	25 6 (42) Shabbath Shabbathon **6th Sabbath** (43) 7
26 (43) (44) 8	27 (44) (45) 9	28 (45) (46) 10	29 (46) (47) 11	30 (47) (48) 12	31 (48) (49) 13th	1 13th (49) June Shabbath Shabbathon **7th Sabbath** **the Feast of Weeks begins @ sunset** no servile work (50) **14th**
2 **14th** (50) **the Feast of Weeks ends @ sunset** no servile work 15	3 16	4 17	5 18	6 19	7 20	8 20 Shabbath Shabbathon 21
9 22	10 23	11 24	12 25	13 26	14 27	15 27 Shabbath Shabbathon 28
16 29	17 30	18 30 4th chodesh / month begins @ sunset 1	19 1			

The 13th is the 7th Sabbath / day 49. The 14th is the 50th day.

June / July ‎ו 4th month 2024

1st Day Sunday	2nd Day Monday	3rd Day Tuesday	4th Day Wednesday	5th Day Thursday	6th Day Friday	Shabbat Saturday
	17 30 30	18 30 June 4th chodesh / month begins @ sunset 1	19 1 2	20 3	21 4	22 4 Shabbath Shabbathon 5
23 6	24 7	25 8	26 9	27 10	28 11	29 11 Shabbath Shabbathon 12
30 13	1 July 14	2 15	3 16	4 17	5 18	6 18 Shabbath Shabbathon 19
7 20	8 21	9 22	10 23	11 24	12 25	13 25 Shabbath Shabbathon 26
14 27	15 28	16 29	17 30	18 30 5th chodesh / month begins @ sunset 1	19 1	

July / August ן 5th month 2024

1st Day Sunday	2nd Day Monday	3rd Day Tuesday	4th Day Wednesday	5th Day Thursday	6th Day Friday	Shabbat Saturday
			17	18 30 July 5th chodesh / month begins @ sunset 1	19 1 2	20 2 Shabbath Shabbathon 3
			30			
21 4	22 5	23 6	24 7	25 8	26 9	27 9 Shabbath Shabbathon 10
28 11	29 12	30 13	31 14	1 August 15	2 16	3 16 Shabbath Shabbathon 17
4 18	5 19	6 20	7 21	8 22	9 23	10 23 Shabbath Shabbathon 24
11 25	12 26	13 27	14 28	15 29	16 30	17 30 6th chodesh / month begins @ sunset 1

_____
_____
_____
_____

August / September   ו   6th month 2024

1st Day Sunday	2nd Day Monday	3rd Day Tuesday	4th Day Wednesday	5th Day Thursday	6th Day Friday	Shabbat Saturday
					16 ... 30	17 ... 30 August ... Shabbath Shabbathon ... 6th chodesh / month begins @ sunset ... 1
18 ... 1 ... 2	19 ... 3	20 ... 4	21 ... 5	22 ... 6	23 ... 7	24 ... 7 ... Shabbath Shabbathon ... 8
25 ... 9	26 ... 10	27 ... 11	28 ... 12	29 ... 13	30 ... 14	31 ... 14 ... Shabbath Shabbathon ... 15
1 September ... 16	2 ... 17	3 ... 18	4 ... 19	5 ... 20	6 ... 21	7 ... 21 ... Shabbath Shabbathon ... 22
8 ... 23	9 ... 24	10 ... 25	11 ... 26	12 ... 27	13 ... 28	14 ... 28 ... 29
15 ... 30	16 ... 30 7th chodesh / month begins @ sunset ... 1					

September / October

Always looking unto Yeshua.

7th month 2024

1st Day Sunday	2nd Day Monday	3rd Day Tuesday	4th Day Wednesday	5th Day Thursday	6th Day Friday	Shabbat Saturday
15 _____ 30	16 _____ 30 September 7th chodesh / month begins @ sunset **the Day of Trumpets / Yom Teruah** begins @ sunset — ends @ sunset **1st** Shabbathon	17 **1st** _____ 2	18 _____ 3	19 _____ 4	20 _____ 5	21 5 Shabbath Shabbathon 6
22 Autumn (Former Rains) Joel 2:23, Jer 5:24, & Dt 11:14 7	23 _____ 8	24 _____ 9	25 **the Day of Atonement / Yom Kippur** begins @ sunset — ends @ sunset **10th** Shabbath Shabbathon 11	26 **10th** _____ 11	27 _____ 12	28 12 Shabbath Shabbathon 13
29 _____ 14	30 _____ 15	1 **15th** October **1st Day of the Feast of Tabernacles** begins @ sunset — ends @ sunset **15th** Shabbathon 16	2 _____ 17	3 _____ 18	4 _____ 19	5 19 Shabbath Shabbathon 20
6 _____ 21	7 _____ 22	8 **22nd** **Last (8th) Day of the Feast of Tabernacles** begins @ sunset — ends @ sunset **22nd** Shabbathon 23	9 _____ 24	10 _____ 25	11 _____ 26	12 26 Shabbath Shabbathon 27
13 _____ 28	14 _____ 29	15 _____ 30	16 30 8th chodesh / month begins @ sunset 1	17 1		

The Feast of Tabernacles is 7 days, and the 8th day is referred to as *the last day, that great [day] of the feast* in John 7:37.

October / November ו 8th month 2024

1st Day Sunday	2nd Day Monday	3rd Day Tuesday	4th Day Wednesday	5th Day Thursday	6th Day Friday	Shabbat Saturday
		15 ⁣ 30	16 30 October 8th chodesh / month begins @ sunset 1	17 1 2	18 3	19 3 Shabbath Shabbathon 4
20 5	21 6	22 7	23 8	24 9	25 10	26 10 Shabbath Shabbathon 11
27 12	28 13	29 14	30 15	31 16	1 November 17	2 17 Shabbath Shabbathon 18
3 19	4 20	5 21	6 22	7 23	8 24	9 24 Shabbath Shabbathon 25
10 26	11 27	12 28	13 29	14 30	15 30 9th chodesh / month begins @ sunset 1	16 1

November / December ן 9th month 2024

1st Day Sunday	2nd Day Monday	3rd Day Tuesday	4th Day Wednesday	5th Day Thursday	6th Day Friday	Shabbat Saturday
				14 30	15 30 November 9th chodesh / month begins @ sunset 1	16 1 Shabbath Shabbathon 2
17 3	18 4	19 5	20 6	21 7	22 8	23 8 Shabbath Shabbathon 9
24 10	25 11	26 12	27 13	28 14	29 15	30 15 Shabbath Shabbathon 16
1 December 17	2 18	3 19	4 20	5 21	6 22	7 22 Shabbath Shabbathon 23
8 24	9 25	10 26	11 27	12 28	13 29	14 29 30

_____
_____
_____
_____

December / January ל 10th month 2024/25

1st Day Sunday	2nd Day Monday	3rd Day Tuesday	4th Day Wednesday	5th Day Thursday	6th Day Friday	Shabbat Saturday
15 30 December 10th chodesh / month begins @ sunset 1	16 1 2	17 3	18 4	19 5	20 6	21 6 Shabbath Shabbathon 7
22 8	23 9	24 10	25 11	26 12	27 13	28 13 Shabbath Shabbathon 14
29 15	30 16	31 17	1 January 18	2 19	3 20	4 20 Shabbath Shabbathon 21
5 22	6 23	7 24	8 25	9 26	10 27	11 27 Shabbath Shabbathon 28
12 29	13 30	14 30 11th chodesh / month begins @ sunset 1	15 1 			

_____

_____

_____

_____

January / February ו 11th month 2025

1st Day Sunday	2nd Day Monday	3rd Day Tuesday	4th Day Wednesday	5th Day Thursday	6th Day Friday	Shabbat Saturday
	13 30 30	14 January 11th chodesh / month begins @ sunset 1	15 1 2	16 3	17 4	18 4 *Shabbath Shabbathon* 5
19 6	20 7	21 8	22 9	23 10	24 11	25 11 *Shabbath Shabbathon* 12
26 13	27 14	28 15	29 16	30 17	31 18	1 18 February *Shabbath Shabbathon* 19
2 20	3 21	4 22	5 23	6 24	7 25	8 25 *Shabbath Shabbathon* 26
9 27	10 28	11 29	12 30	13 30 12th chodesh / month begins @ sunset 1	14 1	

_____

_____

_____

_____

February / March ו 12th month 2025

1st Day Sunday	2nd Day Monday	3rd Day Tuesday	4th Day Wednesday	5th Day Thursday	6th Day Friday	Shabbat Saturday
			12 30	13 30 February 12th chodesh / month begins @ sunset 1	14 1 2	15 2 Shabbath Shabbathon 3
16 4	17 5	18 6	19 7	20 8	21 9	22 9 Shabbath Shabbathon 10
23 11	24 12	25 13	26 14	27 15	28 16	1 16 March Shabbath Shabbathon 17
2 18	3 19	4 20	5 21	6 22	7 23	8 23 Shabbath Shabbathon 24
9 25	10 26	11 27	12 28	13 29	14 30	15 30 time prior to Abib 1 0

As it relates to creation week (before Elohim made the lights in the firmament - Genesis 1:14-19), the time prior to Abib 1 is explained in *What's Up with the New Moon?*

_____

_____

_____

_____

2024 Gregorian Calendar Dates

Passover / April 2nd-3rd

The 1st Day of the Feast of Unleavened Bread / April 3rd-4th

The 7th Day of the Feast of Unleavened Bread / April 9th-10th

Wave-sheaf / April 13th-14th

The Feast of Weeks / June 1st-2nd

The Day of Trumpets / September 16th-17th

The Day of Atonement / September 25th-26th

The 1st Day of the Feast of Tabernacles / September 30th-Oct 1st

The Last (8th) Day of the Feast of Tabernacles / October 7th-8th

The Feast of Tabernacles is 7 days, and the 8th day is referred to
as the last day, that great day of the feast in John 7:37.

March / April

Always looking unto Yeshua.

1st month 2025

1st Day Sunday	2nd Day Monday	3rd Day Tuesday	4th Day Wednesday	5th Day Thursday	6th Day Friday	Shabbat Saturday
23 March 0	24 0	25 0	26 **Abib** Year begins @ sunset 1st chodesh / month 1	27 2	28 Shabbat begins @ sunset 3	29　3 Shabbath Shabbat ends @ sunset 4
30 5	31 6	1 April 7	2 8	3 9	4 10	5　10 Shabbath Shabbathon 11
6 12	7 13	8 **Passover** begins @ sunset ends @ sunset **14th**	9　**14th** Yeshua crucified Yeshua laid in the tomb **1st Day of the Feast of Unleavened Bread** begins @ sunset **15th** no servile work	10　**15th** a night to be much observed Ex 12:42 ends @ sunset 16	11 17	12　**17th** **Yeshua rose from the grave on the Sabbath day** 18
13　**18th** Yeshua appeared to Mary and the disciples 19	14 20	15 **7th Day of the Feast of Unleavened Bread** begins @ sunset **21st** no servile work	16　**21st** ends @ sunset 22	17 23	18 24	19　24 Shabbath Shabbathon (1)　**25th**
20　**25th**　(1) wave-sheaf 8 days later, Yeshua again appeared to the disciples (2)　26	21　count (2) until sunset (3)　27	22　count (3) until sunset (4)　28	23　count (4) until sunset (5)　29	24　count (5) until sunset (6)　30	25　30 count (6) until sunset 2nd chodesh / month begins @ sunset 1	26　1 Morrow after the Sabbath - Begin count @ sunset

count (1) until sunset
count (2) begins @ sunset

Exodus 12:42 It is a night to be much observed unto YHWH...

© 2022/23 FTIH - A Herald

Spring - Thursday, March 20, 2025

Biblical Year Begins - Wednesday, March 26, 2025 (4th day - in the middle of the week)

If Yeshua tarries...

Spring - Friday, March 20, 2026 9:46am CDT / Friday March 20, 2026 4:46pm IST (Israel Standard Time)

Biblical Year Begins - Wednesday, March 25, 2026

Spring - Saturday, March 20, 2027 3:25pm CDT / Saturday March 20, 2027 10:25pm IST (Israel Standard Time)

Biblical Year Begins - Wednesday, March 24, 2027

Spring - Sunday, March 19, 2028 9:17pm CDT / Monday, March 20, 2028 4:17am IST (Israel Standard Time)

Biblical Year Begins - Wednesday, March 22, 2028

Spring - Tuesday, March 20, 2029 3:02am CDT / Tuesday, March 20, 2029 10:02am IST (Israel Standard Time)

Biblical Year Begins - Wednesday, March 21, 2029

Spring - Wednesday, March 20, 2030 8:52am CDT / Wednesday March 20, 2030 3:52pm IST (Israel Standard Time)

Biblical Year Begins - Wednesday, March 20, 2030

Spring begins at 3:52pm IST prior to sunset, thus the biblical year begins on Wednesday, March 20, 2030 at sunset.

For Your Information:

Gregorian Leap Years (1 day added / February 29th): 2024, 2028

Jewish Leap Years (29 days added / Adar II): 5784 (2024), 5787 (2027), 5790 (2030)

Extra Calendars - months/years
(waiting for the return of Yeshua Messiah)

March / April

Always looking unto Yeshua.

1st Day Sunday	2nd Day Monday	3rd Day Tuesday	4th Day Wednesday	5th Day Thursday	6th Day Friday	Shabbat Saturday
			Abib Year begins @ sunset 1st chodesh / month 1	2	Shabbat begins @ sunset 3	3 Shabbath Shabbathon Shabbat ends @ sunset 4
5	6	7	8	9	10	10 Shabbath Shabbathon 11
12	13	**14th** Passover begins @ sunset ends @ sunset **14th**	**14th** Yeshua crucified Yeshua laid in the tomb 1st Day of the Feast of Unleavened Bread begins @ sunset **15th** no servile work	**15th** a night to be much observed Ex 12:42 ends @ sunset 16	17	**17th** Yeshua rose from the grave on the Sabbath day Shabbath Shabbathon 18
18th Yeshua appeared to Mary and the disciples 19	20	**21st** 7th Day of the Feast of Unleavened Bread begins @ sunset **21st** no servile work	**21st** ends @ sunset 22	23	24	24 Shabbath Shabbathon (1) **25th**
25th (1) wave-sheaf 8 days later, Yeshua again appeared to the disciples (2) 26	count (2) until sunset (3) 27	count (3) until sunset (4) 28	count (4) until sunset (5) 29	count (5) until sunset (6) 30	30 count (6) until sunset 2nd chodesh / month begins @ sunset 1	1 Morrow after the Sabbath - Begin count @ sunset

count (1) until sunset
count (2) begins @ sunset

Exodus 12:42 It is a night to be much observed unto YHWH...

© 2022 FTIH - A Herald

April / May

ו

2nd month ____

1st Day Sunday	2nd Day Monday	3rd Day Tuesday	4th Day Wednesday	5th Day Thursday	6th Day Friday	Shabbat Saturday
			Begin counting the Sabbaths ⟶		30	1 count (7) until sunset **1st Sabbath** Shabbathon
				30	2nd chodesh / month begins @ sunset (7) 1	(8) 2
(8) (9) 3	(9) (10) 4	(10) (11) 5	(11) (12) 6	(12) (13) 7	(13) (14) 8	8 (14) **2nd Sabbath** Shabbathon (15) 9
(15) (16) 10	(16) (17) 11	(17) (18) 12	(18) (19) 13	(19) (20) 14	(20) (21) 15	15 (21) **3rd Sabbath** Shabbathon (22) 16
(22) (23) 17	(23) (24) 18	(24) (25) 19	(25) (26) 20	(26) (27) 21	(27) (28) 22	22 (28) **4th Sabbath** Shabbathon (29) 23
(29) (30) 24	(30) (31) 25	(31) (32) 26	(32) (33) 27	(33) (34) 28	(34) (35) 29	29 (35) **5th Sabbath** Shabbathon (36) 30

May / June

Always looking unto Yeshua.

3rd month ____

1st Day Sunday	2nd Day Monday	3rd Day Tuesday	4th Day Wednesday	5th Day Thursday	6th Day Friday	Shabbat Saturday
30 (36) 3rd chodesh / month begins @ sunset (37) 1	1 (37) (38) 2	(38) (39) 3	(39) (40) 4	(40) (41) 5	(41) (42) 6	6 (42) **6th Sabbath** Shabbath Shabbathon (43) 7
(43) (44) 8	(44) (45) 9	(45) (46) 10	(46) (47) 11	(47) (48) 12	(48) (49) 13th	13th (49) **7th Sabbath the Feast of Weeks begins @ sunset** no servile work (50) **14th**
14th (50) **the Feast of Weeks ends @ sunset** no servile work 15	16	17	18	19	20	20 Shabbath Shabbathon 21
22	23	24	25	26	27	27 Shabbath Shabbathon 28
29	30	30 4th chodesh / month begins @ sunset 1	1			

The 13th is the 7th Sabbath / day 49. The 14th is the 50th day.   © 2022 FTIH - A Herald

_____
_____
_____
_____

35

June / July ו 4th month ____

1st Day Sunday	2nd Day Monday	3rd Day Tuesday	4th Day Wednesday	5th Day Thursday	6th Day Friday	Shabbat Saturday
		30 4th chodesh / month begins @ sunset 1	1 2	 3	 4	4 *Shabbath Shabbathon* 5
6	7	8	9	10	11	11 *Shabbath Shabbathon* 12
13	14	15	16	17	18	18 *Shabbath Shabbathon* 19
20	21	22	23	24	25	25 *Shabbath Shabbathon* 26
27	28	29	30	30 5th chodesh / month begins @ sunset 1	1	

_____

_____

_____

_____

July / August   ו   5th month ____

1st Day Sunday	2nd Day Monday	3rd Day Tuesday	4th Day Wednesday	5th Day Thursday	6th Day Friday	Shabbat Saturday
			30 30	30 5th chodesh / month begins @ sunset 1	1 2	2 Shabbath Shabbathon 3
4	5	6	7	8	9	9 Shabbath Shabbathon 10
11	12	13	14	15	16	16 Shabbath Shabbathon 17
18	19	20	21	22	23	23 Shabbath Shabbathon 24
25	26	27	28	29	30	30 6th chodesh / month begins @ sunset 1

_____
_____
_____
_____

August / September ו 6th month ____

1st Day Sunday	2nd Day Monday	3rd Day Tuesday	4th Day Wednesday	5th Day Thursday	6th Day Friday	Shabbat Saturday
					30	30 Shabbath Shabbathon 6th chodesh / month begins @ sunset 1
1 2	3	4	5	6	7	7 Shabbath Shabbathon 8
9	10	11	12	13	14	14 Shabbath Shabbathon 15
16	17	18	19	20	21	21 Shabbath Shabbathon 22
23 30	24 30 7th chodesh / month begins @ sunset 1	25	26	27	28	28 29

_____
_____
_____
_____

September / October

Always looking unto Yeshua. **7th month** ____

1st Day Sunday	2nd Day Monday	3rd Day Tuesday	4th Day Wednesday	5th Day Thursday	6th Day Friday	Shabbat Saturday
	30	**1st**				5
	7th chodesh / month begins @ sunset **the Day of Trumpets / Yom Teruah** begins @ sunset ends @ sunset					Shabbath Shabbathon
30	**1st** Shabbathon	2	3	4	5	6
				10th		12
			the Day of Atonement / Yom Kippur begins @ sunset ends @ sunset			Shabbath Shabbathon
7	8	9	**10th** Shabbath Shabbathon 11	12		13
		15th				19
		1st Day of the Feast of Tabernacles begins @ sunset ends @ sunset				Shabbath Shabbathon
14		**15th** Shabbathon 16	17	18	19	20
		22nd				26
		Last (8th) Day of the Feast of Tabernacles begins @ sunset ends @ sunset				Shabbath Shabbathon
21		**22nd** Shabbathon 23	24	25	26	27
			30	20 1		
			8th chodesh / month begins @ sunset			
28	29	30	1			

The Feast of Tabernacles is 7 days, and the 8th day is referred to as *the last day, that great [day] of the feast* in John 7:37.

© 2022 FTIH - A Herald

_____
_____
_____
_____

October / November ו 8th month ____

1st Day Sunday	2nd Day Monday	3rd Day Tuesday	4th Day Wednesday	5th Day Thursday	6th Day Friday	Shabbat Saturday
		30 30	30 8th chodesh / month begins @ sunset 1	1 2	3	3 Shabbath Shabbathon 4
5	6	7	8	9	10	10 Shabbath Shabbathon 11
12	13	14	15	16	17	17 Shabbath Shabbathon 18
19	20	21	22	23	24	24 Shabbath Shabbathon 25
26	27	28	29	30	30 9th chodesh / month begins @ sunset 1	1

_____

_____

_____

_____

November / December ו 9th month ____

1st Day Sunday	2nd Day Monday	3rd Day Tuesday	4th Day Wednesday	5th Day Thursday	6th Day Friday	Shabbat Saturday
				30	30 9th chodesh / month begins @ sunset 1	1 Shabbath Shabbathon 2
3	4	5	6	7	8	8 Shabbath Shabbathon 9
10	11	12	13	14	15	15 Shabbath Shabbathon 16
17	18	19	20	21	22	22 Shabbath Shabbathon 23
24	25	26	27	28	29	29 30

_____
_____
_____
_____

December / January ו 10th month _____

1st Day Sunday	2nd Day Monday	3rd Day Tuesday	4th Day Wednesday	5th Day Thursday	6th Day Friday	Shabbat Saturday
30 10th chodesh / month begins @ sunset 1	1 2	 3	 4	 5	 6	6 Shabbath Shabbathon 7
   8	 9	 10	 11	 12	 13	13 Shabbath Shabbathon 14
   15	 16	 17	 18	 19	 20	20 Shabbath Shabbathon 21
   22	 23	 24	 25	 26	 27	27 Shabbath Shabbathon 28
   29	 30	30 11th chodesh / month begins @ sunset 1	1			

_____
_____
_____
_____

January / February ו 11th month _____

1st Day Sunday	2nd Day Monday	3rd Day Tuesday	4th Day Wednesday	5th Day Thursday	6th Day Friday	Shabbat Saturday
	30	30 11th chodesh / month begins @ sunset 1	1 2	3	4	4 *Shabbath Shabbathon* 5
6	7	8	9	10	11	11 *Shabbath Shabbathon* 12
13	14	15	16	17	18	18 *Shabbath Shabbathon* 19
20	21	22	23	24	25	25 *Shabbath Shabbathon* 26
27	28	29	30	30 12th chodesh / month begins @ sunset 1	1	

_____

_____

_____

_____

February / March ן 12th month _____

1st Day Sunday	2nd Day Monday	3rd Day Tuesday	4th Day Wednesday	5th Day Thursday	6th Day Friday	Shabbat Saturday
			30	30 12th chodesh / month begins @ sunset 1	1 2	2 *Shabbath Shabbathon* 3
4	5	6	7	8	9	9 *Shabbath Shabbathon* 10
11	12	13	14	15	16	16 *Shabbath Shabbathon* 17
18	19	20	21	22	23	23 *Shabbath Shabbathon* 24
25	26	27	28	29	30	30 time prior to Abib 1 0

_____
_____
_____
_____

Resources

Strong's Exhaustive Concordance
Brown-Driver-Briggs Hebrew Lexicon
Thayer's Greek Lexicon
The Berean Interlinear
The Interlinear Hebrew-Greek-English Bible with
Strong's Concordance
NAS Exhaustive Concordance
Ancient Hebrew Learning Center
BibleHub.com
BlueLetterBible.org
King James Bible

Habakkuk 2:4 ...the just shall live by his faith (emunah).

Psalm 96:13 Before YHWH: for he cometh, for he cometh to judge the earth: he shall judge the world with righteousness, and the people with his truth (emunah).

Luke 18:8 ...when the Son of man cometh, shall he find faith on the earth?

For the Reader

Yahweh bless thee, and keep thee: Yahweh make his face shine upon thee, and be gracious unto thee: Yahweh lift up his countenance upon thee, and give thee peace.
Numbers 6:24-26

Other Titles

What's Up With The New Moon?
No Lesser Light is Going to Rule His Days!
This book is a comprehensive study that methodically breaks down:
When the biblical year begins.
In which months are the Feasts.
The difference between Feast Days, Appointed Times, Holy Convocations, and Sabbaths.
Spreadsheets and calendars included.

Faith That Is His:
When Your Belief is Heavy, His Faith is Light.
A book challenging mainstream teachings on faith as well as other religious doctrines.
Some questions this book answers:
What is (His) faith?
What is grace?
Did Yeshua die on Good Friday?
Did Yeshua rise on Easter Sunday?
Was Yeshua in the grave for two days or three?
Who is the thief in John 10:10?

Divorced:
The Church Forbids reMarriage, but According to the Bible, You are Free to Marry.
Some topics this book covers are:
The difference between divorce and separation.
The true meaning of adultery.
The explanation of the Law of Divorce.
Can the ex-spouse live?
Returning to a former spouse.
Who has authority?

Connect With Us

Faith That is His – A Herald
(Heralding the Messiah)

A messianic resource created to share the Good News of the Kingdom and to announce and help prepare for the soon return of Yeshua the Messiah. Our purpose is to do the works of the Kingdom by providing resources through books, teachings, and study guides. As we are able, our goal is to provide these resources free of charge.

To learn more about our publishing company please visit FaithThatIsHis.com.

Faith on the Earth Ministries
(Proclaiming the Faith of Yeshua Messiah)

As a messianic ministry, we share some of the same beliefs as Christianity (death, burial, resurrection, and return of Yeshua), but we also share some of the same beliefs as Judaism (Elohim is One, keeping the Commandments and the Holy Days found in Scripture). Darker days are coming upon this world and times will go from bad to worse and from worse to the unthinkable and unimaginable. As such, we exist to, warn the people, call them to repentance, and point them back to Yahweh.

To learn more about our ministry please visit FaithOnTheEarth.org

Sound of the Shofar

Can you hear that sound? The sound of the shofar.

It's the voice of the Almighty.

He's calling His people. *Return unto Me*, are His words.

Isaiah (Yeshayah/Yeshayahu) 44:22

Made in United States
Troutdale, OR
09/29/2024

23230076R00038